SWIMMING LESSONS

The Story of Jonah

Dr. Joseph Davis

renownpublishing

Renown Publishing
www.renownpublishing.com

Swimming Lessons / Joseph Davis
ISBN-13: 978-1-952602-91-7

CONTENTS

Is Your Love for God's Word Selective?

God's word can have a polarizing effect on our hearts. By this I mean we tend to have one of two reactions to His word: either we love a given scripture, or we wish it weren't there. You can probably think of scriptural themes or favorite verses you enjoy reading or hearing about. They're comforting, encouraging, and uplifting.

Evidence of this trend is abundant on social media, where you can see posts of verses filled with promises and encouragement, like these:

> ¹¹*You make known to me the path of life; in your presence there is fullness of joy; at your right hand are pleasures forevermore.*
>
> **—Psalm 16:11**

16For God so loved the world, that he gave his only Son, that whoever believes in him should not perish but have eternal life.

—John 3:16

13I can do all things through him who strengthens me.
—Philippians 4:13

Aren't those verses uplifting? Of course, if we're feeling edgy, there is the occasional command from God we "like" on our social media feeds:

39...You shall love your neighbor as yourself.
—Matthew 22:39

We all have our favorite scriptures. There's nothing wrong with clinging to encouraging and inspirational words from God, but what about the other scriptures? You know: the parts of the Bible most of us prefer to ignore or even wish didn't exist. When we come to those or hear someone preach on them, we get really quiet, really fast.

For instance, you don't see many social media memes about the stern warnings from Old Testament prophets. You don't see many professional athletes sporting scripture references from Leviticus on their cheeks. We tend to neglect many passages that, if God really means what He says, make it clear we must make significant changes in our lives. Maybe they address specific sins, things we shouldn't be doing but don't want to stop or don't think we can afford to stop. Maybe we avoid Scripture that speaks to our sexual purity, how our marriages function, or how we manage money.

Even if we don't completely ignore these verses, we hope God intends them to be suggestions, not commands. When the passages clearly appear to be written as commands, we hope He is speaking hypothetically. One way or another, we rationalize away the scriptures we don't like, if we even acknowledge their existence at all. Why? So we can move on with our lives. We quickly run back to the parts of God's word we prefer—to Psalm 16, John 3:16, and Philippians 4:13.

Where does that leave us? Perhaps more comfortable, yes. However, it's also a place of disobedience. Disobedience is precisely what the book of Jonah is about. Jonah was a prophet who, like us, loved some of God's word but not all of it. Together, we will look at Jonah's story from historical, spiritual, and personal perspectives. We will explore the hard lessons Jonah learned about grace, judgment, and repentance. Hopefully, we will each learn, or relearn, something about the benefits of swimming in obedience, instead of disobedience, to God.

Hoarding Grace

Let's begin our study of Jonah with some historical context. The story of Jonah is dated to somewhere in the early or mid-eighth century B.C., possibly around 760 B.C. [1] The nation of Israel was divided between northern and southern kingdoms. Jonah was a prophet during the reign of Jeroboam II (which lasted from 793 or so to 753 B.C.) [2] in the northern kingdom. Although Jeroboam wasn't a righteous king (2 Kings 14:23–24), he was a competent one. The northern kingdom prospered economically under his rule. [3] Yet there was an unmistakable undercurrent of spiritual rebellion in those years, as Israel failed to serve as a light for God's truth to the pagan world.

Israel had a long-standing rivalry with its neighbor Assyria, in modern-day Iraq. There was no love lost, no exchange of warm, fuzzy feelings between these nations. They shared a perpetual, mutual history replete with invasions, battles, and bloodshed, as documented in 2 Kings,

2 Chronicles, and other books of the Old Testament. The prophets Hosea and Amos, contemporaries of Jonah, declared if Israel (the northern kingdom) refused to repent, God would allow Assyria to conquer and enslave them.

> *⁵They shall not return to the land of Egypt, but Assyria shall be their king, because they have refused to return to me.*
> **—Hosea 11:5**

This was a central theme throughout their ministry as prophets. Any Israelites who listened to the prophets of God knew, sooner or later, the Lord would use Assyria to judge Israel. It seemed it was just a matter of time.

In fact, this prophecy from Hosea came to fruition thirty years later, in 722 B.C. [4] In the meantime, Jews in the northern kingdom held a natural, visceral disdain for and fear of the Assyrians. After all, Assyria represented the greatest earthly threat to the prosperity of God's people. Assyria was, no doubt, their greatest geopolitical foe.

This is where Jonah enters the story. He receives instructions from God to take a message of repentance, not to his fellow Israelites, but to Nineveh, the capital of the Assyrian empire!

> *¹Now the word of the LORD came to Jonah the son of Amittai, saying, ²"Arise, go to Nineveh, that great city, and call out against it, for their evil has come up before me." ³But Jonah rose to flee to Tarshish from the presence of the LORD. He went down to Joppa and found a ship going to Tarshish. So*

he paid the fare and went down into it, to go with them to
Tarshish, away from the presence of the Lord.

—Jonah 1:1–3

HISTORICAL: JONAH HATES NINEVEH

This isn't the first time the Lord calls Jonah to preach repentance to others, and Jonah has always been obedient before. However, this time, Jonah responds with immediate, blatant disobedience to God's command to go to Nineveh and preach repentance. What's the difference this time around?

Fun Obedience

Although Jonah is a prophet of the Lord, he is also a patriotic Israelite. Like most of his countrymen, Jonah believes—or, rather, he assumes—Israel is meant to be the sole beneficiary of God's blessings. If you read about the time when God gives Jonah a glorious, victorious prophecy for King Jeroboam, you can see Jonah's deep patriotic passion for his country. It's recorded in the only Old Testament mention of Jonah outside of the book bearing his name:

> 25He restored the border of Israel from Lebo-hamath as far as the Sea of the Arabah, according to the word of the Lord, the God of Israel, which he spoke by his servant Jonah the son of Amittai, the prophet, who was from Gath-hepher. 26For the Lord saw that the affliction of Israel was very bitter, for there was none left, bond or free, and there was

3

> none to help Israel. ²⁷But the LORD had not said that he
> would blot out the name of Israel from under heaven, so he
> saved them by the hand of Jeroboam the son of Joash.
> —*2 Kings 14:25–27*

Do you think patriotic Jonah enjoys delivering this prophecy from 2 Kings to his fellow Israelites and his king? Jonah is likely thrilled to share it! What prophet wouldn't want to be the bearer of good tidings? When God says, "Tell your disobedient leader I am going to bless his reign anyway," a patriot would have no problem delivering *that* word from the Lord. Any prophet of God would be eager to share the message of God's grace and undeserved favor with whomever God wants to hear it. God's grace is exciting! It's fun to tell people the kind of news they want to hear.

Nineveh Was Ready

Assyria wasn't without its problems during that time: there were famines, internal revolts, and a devastating earthquake. ⁵ It was a nation experiencing what many people at the time would have seen as omens of divine judgment. This pagan nation had been brought to a place of desperation, with hearts prepared by the grace of God to hear the word of God. The nation of Assyria was ripe for a message from the Lord warning of the consequences of evil and offering the promises of forgiveness through repentance. That job fell to Jonah, and Jonah had a problem with it.

Selfish Prophet

Why would Jonah, given his natural attachment to his people and hatred of their enemies, want to preach a message that said Assyria would receive the blessings from God he believed should belong to Israel alone? Besides, it was a very long, difficult journey to Nineveh. Jonah realized he would be stuck there for a while. God wasn't calling him to present the gospel at a weekend conference. This journey would take months, maybe years. What about his family? What kind of father would he be, exposing his kids to the wickedness of Assyrian culture?

Beyond that, what kind of Israelite would want to spend any time in Nineveh? There was no temple for sacrificing to the Lord, only places of pagan worship and idols. As far as Jonah was concerned, Nineveh wasn't good for anything except disgusting food, strange music, and lack of good fashion sense.

Then there was the political reality: Assyria was Israel's biggest threat, right next door. Jonah had no desire to make Assyrians part of his life, and the kingdom of Israel had no desire to build community or common ground with Assyria. The last thing Jonah or any Israelite wanted politically was an obedient Assyria sharing in the blessings promised to Israel. In fact, Israel had enjoyed for years what seemed to be God's judgment on the Assyrians for doing evil, even as Jonah delivered his favorite prophecy ever: that God would be letting Israel skate by with grace and blessings they didn't deserve! *"Wait, I'm supposed to go to Nineveh and preach to Assyrians so they can be forgiven and receive blessings—our blessings no less? No way,"* Jonah was surely thinking.

So Jonah did what any rational, Assyria-hating prophet of God would do: he pretended he hadn't heard the Lord's command. In fact, he headed 180 degrees in the opposite direction of Nineveh (near present-day Mosul, Iraq) to the port of Tarshish (in present-day Spain). Jonah wanted to hoard God's grace. In fact, this cycle of hoarding God's grace wasn't unique to Jonah; it had become a consistent, corporate, nationwide spiritual and moral failure of the nation of Israel.

SPIRITUAL: SAVING PAGANS

²And I will make of you a great nation, and I will bless you and make your name great, so that you will be a blessing. ³I will bless those who bless you, and him who dishonors you I will curse, and in you all the families of the earth shall be blessed.

—Genesis 12:2–3

Despite what Jonah and his countrymen believed, God never intended grace to be hoarded by Israel. In fact, God expected His people to take His message to Gentile nations! When God called Jonah to preach to the Assyrians in their capital, it wasn't some random command, some frivolous test. God's calling for Jonah was part of a direct, sovereign act of grace to a foreign, pagan people—hundreds of years before Jesus gave us the Great Commission to "go therefore and make disciples of all nations" (Matthew 28:19).

As we begin the book of Jonah, we see God is ready to bless Assyria with a message of redemption, forgiveness, and hope through His prophet. Since God wants to save the Assyrians, He strategically sends Jonah to preach in Nineveh, their seat of power and influence. This isn't God sending Jonah some petty test to see how good of a prophet he is. Jonah is God's chosen preacher for an important mission!

Jonah's Unwilling Feet

> *13For "everyone who calls on the name of the Lord will be saved." 14How then will they call on him in whom they have not believed? And how are they to believe in him of whom they have never heard? And how are they to hear without someone preaching? 15And how are they to preach unless they are sent? As it is written, "How beautiful are the feet of those who preach the good news!"*
> **—Romans 10:13–15**

God sending Jonah to deliver His word to Nineveh is not a spur-of-the-moment whim. It has been part of His overall plan from the beginning, and it foreshadows the Great Commission. Through the centuries, always and to this day, God expands His kingdom through the feet and lips of His children.

But Jonah has no intention of being "beautiful feet" upon the mountains. He has no desire to bring the good news to Nineveh. He wants nothing to do with any of it. This is a "no-fun" kind of commission from the Lord. "Beautiful feet" start with someone willing to go, to preach, and to teach, but Jonah is not willing. When it comes to Nineveh, Jonah prefers ugly shoes in Spain to beautiful feet in the land of the Assyrians.

PERSONAL: UGLY SHOES

It's easy for us to shake our heads at Jonah, but we're no better. We tend to have the same kind of reaction to God in our daily lives. The truth is *our human nature and instinct is to be consumers of grace rather than conduits for it.*

Selective Obedience

Have you ever pretended you couldn't hear someone because you didn't like what the person was saying or thought you wouldn't like what the person was about to say? Maybe it was your boss, a colleague, or a friend. Many of us attempted this trick with our parents when we were children, even if it probably didn't fool them for a second. Of course, we'd never try any such deception with our spouse—right?

Yet people come to church and do this all the time with God's word. On a regular basis, we ignore or neglect the wisdom and commands of Scripture. We politely nod and then procrastinate on making any changes in our lives until it completely slips our minds. Too often, we try to fake our obedience to the word of God.

What commands from God are you selective about? Which ones do you find it easier simply to ignore, pretending you didn't hear?

Consider for a moment that selective obedience is not obedience at all. From Jonah's story, we can see that selective obedience, at the end of the day, looks like selfishly and deliberately running in the wrong direction, choosing ugly shoes over beautiful feet. What do your feet look like right now? Where are they pointed, toward Nineveh or Tarshish?

Are You Hoarding Grace?

We love the blessings of knowing God, but too often, our daily priorities reveal we're sadly quite selfish with grace. We are most comfortable hoarding grace, barely entertaining any notions of the sacrifice needed to share grace with those around us. Sadly, it's not just Jonah, and it's not just you and I. Most of the American church experience is designed to hoard God's grace. We hoard it for our church and our families, operating on the assumption that our programs, our worship, and our budgets are for us, not for Nineveh.

Oh, we will share grace when it's convenient and it aligns with whatever destination we have in life. We're more than willing to be part of God's process until there's significant cost involved, especially if the cost hinders our personal agenda. Maybe our agenda is as small as our sleep schedule or our Starbucks budget; maybe it includes addictions or the secret sins of our hearts. When we act this way, holding God's goodness so close to the chest, we find ourselves rarely sharing grace with anyone outside our own families, and sometimes we can't even bring ourselves to do that much!

Consequently, many of us end up like Jonah, choosing to wear ugly shoes and trying to put as much distance as possible between us and the place of real obedience to God's instruction and expectations. For this reason, many people prefer to hide in churches adept at handing out pairs of comfortable yet ugly shoes. Instead of learning generous grace, we'd rather just enjoy "our" grace with our friends.

Generous Grace

What would we say are the greatest benefits of grace? Forgiveness and eternal life. Of course, the powerful transformation we experience from His work of grace in us is another benefit. Yes, grace brings us all these things, but if the only way we view grace is in terms of what we receive, then we have become grace-hoarders, like Jonah and the people of Israel. If we're truly receiving God's grace, it inspires generosity, a willingness to share grace with others, even at a cost to ourselves and our personal desires. True grace enables us to see those sacrifices as a privilege, not as a burden to run from, like Jonah ran. Grace is what empowers and emboldens us to go obediently wherever God has called us, even if it means trekking to our own personal Nineveh.

Eventually, we realize we will miss out on the greatest joys life can offer if we are not generous with the grace given to us. That blessedly happy, materially abundant life we seek within the safe shelter of a church will be sadly deficient when life gets stormy. Hoarding grace won't spare us from seasons of difficulty; it will make them worse.

What if the Jonah in your life, the person God called to share grace with you, had hoarded it instead? Quite possibly, he or she did at first, so what if God never let your Jonah experience the consequences of swimming in an ocean of disobedience? You wouldn't even have the chance to hoard grace today if God hadn't relentlessly called that person to carry the gospel obediently with beautiful feet in lieu of living selfishly in ugly shoes.

Are you fighting to keep your head above water in a stormy sea? Are you wondering how you got to this point: *"How did I end up here?"*

It's time to be honest with ourselves and with God and admit we are not as generous as we should be with the grace God has given us. As a result, some of us are drowning in a sea of consequences, learning tough lessons about our disobedience. Oh, don't get me wrong: we're still forgiven, still connected to the Father. But there are real consequences when we hoard grace. Let's not sugarcoat our lack of generosity. Willfully ignoring God's calling is disobedience, and that disobedience always has consequences. We've all been there, and we've all faced the fallout.

If you're finding it hard to swim in the stormy sea of life and you just can't understand why it's so difficult, perhaps it's your selective obedience. The good news is even those swimming lessons are part of God's grace! As we continue with Jonah's story, I encourage you to see these swimming lessons as opportunities to learn to view obedience as a privilege, not a burden. God wants us to crave beautiful feet more than selfishly comfortable, ugly shoes. God wants us to be generous with His grace, not hoard it for ourselves!

Chapter One Questions

Question: Has there ever been something you knew God wanted you to do that made you uncomfortable or was difficult to obey? How did you respond?

_____

_____

_____

_____

_____

_____

_____

_____

_____

_____

_____

Question: Think of a time when you deliberately went against what you knew God wanted you to do (either from His word or through the Holy Spirit). How did you know you were being disobedient? Did you ever correct your course? Why or why not?

_____

_____

_____

_____

_____

_____

_____

_____

_____

_____

Question: What commands from God are you selective about? Which ones do you find are easier simply to ignore, pretending you didn't hear?

_____

_____

_____

_____

_____

_____

_____

_____

_____

_____

_____

Action: Consider for a moment that selective obedience is not obedience at all. If you sense your feet are pointed in the wrong direction (toward complete or partial disobedience rather than complete obedience), spend some time asking the Holy Spirit to work on your heart, reveal to you the joy of obedience, and give you the courage to take steps of change. It may be helpful to make a list of the benefits of grace and the blessings of God's transformative work in your life. What are some practical ways you can extend grace toward others?

Chapter One Notes

_____

_____

_____

_____

_____

_____

_____

_____

_____

_____

_____

_____

_____

_____

_____

_____

God Will Find You

²³Am I a God at hand, declares the Lᴏʀᴅ, and not a God far away? ²⁴Can a man hide himself in secret places so that I cannot see him? declares the Lᴏʀᴅ. Do I not fill heaven and earth? declares the Lᴏʀᴅ.

—Jeremiah 23:23–24

When you read those words of our Lord, how do they strike you? Do they sound ominous? Does His omnipresence intimidate you? Is our inability to evade His sight frightening?

The reality is we cannot hide our sins from God, not one of them. This truth is daunting. When you realize you can't keep even your most intimate, deeply buried sins and secrets from God, it can be overwhelming. The Lord is so omnipresent He is even in our minds and knows our thoughts! Nothing is private from Him.

But we still try to hide from God. We manipulate ourselves into feeling ignorantly comfortable in our disobedience. If we put on blinders so we can't see our sin, then God can't see our sin, either—right? *Wrong.*

Do you remember the last time someone caught you doing something you didn't want anyone to know about, something you had successfully kept from everyone up to that point? Maybe it was something from long ago, and even you had forgotten about it. Perhaps a habitual sinful failure became public, and the consequences were embarrassing or life-altering, even devastating. Maybe it wasn't something you did, but something you were supposed to do but chose not to. In that case, you might have decided obedience would have been too costly, too inconvenient.

Yes, you know nothing is hidden from God, no disobedience or failure to act. However, you continue with life as if God didn't see anything. Eventually time passes, and you get over the initial shame and guilt. It can feel as though you have gotten away with it. That's probably what Jonah is thinking on the ship to Tarshish.

> ⁴But the LORD hurled a great wind upon the sea, and there was a mighty tempest on the sea, so that the ship threatened to break up. ⁵Then the mariners were afraid, and each cried out to his god. And they hurled the cargo that was in the ship into the sea to lighten it for them. But Jonah had gone down into the inner part of the ship and had lain down and was fast asleep. ⁶So the captain came and said to him, "What do you mean, you sleeper? Arise, call out to your god! Perhaps the god will give a thought to us, that we may not perish."
>
> **—Jonah 1:4–6**

HISTORICAL: WHERE IS JONAH?

The Hiding Prophet

When Jonah boards the ship, he goes down to the safest, most secluded section: the lower middle deck. If you want smooth sailing, comfort, and privacy—in short, to stay hidden—that's where you want to be.

The lower middle deck is quiet and isolated. It's dark, and there is little noise from the crew. When the sea is rough, a passenger on this deck feels it the least. This is precisely what Jonah wants, right? The wayward prophet desires isolation and a place to sulk as he hides from God's calling to go to Nineveh. Like us, Jonah craves a place to isolate himself and do what he wants to do. He still believes in God, but he doesn't want to do what God has called him to do. Jonah wants to express his faith in his own, comfortable way to whom he wants, when he wants. Feeling safe and secure in his hiding place, Jonah falls asleep quickly, before the journey has even really started.

A Mysterious Storm

Suddenly, out of nowhere, hurricane-force winds arise. This isn't a little storm or a brief squall; it's an unusual weather event for the area. It's the worst storm these seasoned sailors have ever experienced!

They are on a well-traveled shipping route they have traversed a hundred times. They are completely prepared for the normal weather patterns, but this storm is out of the ordinary. It's big enough for there to have been obvious signs on the horizon. The sailors would have been able to see a storm of this magnitude coming, and they never would have gone out on the water. Jonah 1:13 tells us they try to row back to dry land, suggesting the ship is still fairly close to shore. All of this evidence points to the fact this storm comes out of nowhere and moves in on them quickly.

Since any seasoned first-century mariner could easily spot a storm this massive heading his way, we can surmise, as the sailors do, this is a supernatural weather event. Realizing as much, the ship's crew is looking for an explanation: "Why is this happening? Where did it come from? This isn't normal!"

"The Gods Are Angry"

Given the terrifying and extraordinary nature of the storm, the sailors conclude, "This has been caused by someone on board being judged." Fearing imminent death, the crew begins to cry out to the nonexistent higher powers they worship. Of course, nothing works.

They quickly turn to survival mode, lightening the ship's load and battening down to ride out the storm. They go below deck to jettison cargo. There they discover Jonah, sleeping through the terror! The sailors are dumbfounded Jonah doesn't comprehend the physical and spiritual peril they all face. Ironically, these pagan sailors are more in touch with what is happening spiritually than Jonah is.

The captain exclaims, in effect, "What do you think

you're doing, sleepyhead?" (Well, he may be using less-polite, more-"sailorish" language, but you get the gist.) "How can you sleep at a time like this? We're in danger! Why aren't you praying? Don't you know we're desperate? Whoever your God is, ask Him to save us, because none of ours are listening!"

SPIRITUAL: HURRICANE GRACE

Let's just say it: Jonah is a horrible prophet. He prefers bitterness, self-pity, and victimhood over obedience to the assignment God has given him. We can imagine Jonah complaining, "If God hadn't asked this unreasonable and unfair thing of me, I wouldn't have to hide on this ship!"

Jonah is also a bigot who hates Assyrians more than he loves the Lord, which he reveals when he ignores God's word because it might benefit Israel's enemies.

Overall, Jonah is about as far from the image of Jesus as a prophet can get, huddled in the bowels of a ship in a vain attempt to hide from God.

What Jonah Deserves

Jonah may consider himself more important to God than the Ninevites or superior to the pagan sailors, but God's actions prove He cares about all of them, including the disobedient prophet. It's easy to look at the storm and say, "Wow, God sure is angry at Jonah!"

At first glance, this seems to be a logical interpretation of the story. God gives Jonah an amazing privilege by calling him to Nineveh, but Jonah doesn't want it. Well, then, God should just move on from Jonah, right? It isn't as if God needs Jonah. After all, He is God, and He can pick any prophet He wants. The way Jonah is acting, he doesn't even deserve to be a prophet!

This storm may seem like the right move on God's part to punish Jonah for his disobedience, as if to say, "You think you can hide from Me? I'll teach you!" Jonah certainly deserves God's wrath, doesn't he? If that's what we think, we have another thing coming.

> [10]*For the Son of Man came to seek and to save the lost.*
> —*Luke 19:10*

The wrath of God brings death, not restoration. As it turns out, this storm isn't wrath. That isn't what's happening to Jonah, the ship, and its crew. Wrath and judgment are not how God ultimately deals with His children whom He has chosen to save by faith. He would eventually demonstrate this by sending His Son to take His wrath upon Himself on the cross, where He died on our behalf. This storm is the opposite of wrath; it's grace!

God has no intention of killing Jonah. God also has no intention of letting Jonah remain disobedient to what He has called him to do. No matter how hard Jonah tries to evade what he has been called to do, God is going to do whatever is necessary to wake up His prophet and flush him out of hiding. Why? Because God intends to restore Jonah, despite his callous, rebellious attitude toward God's calling.

Why God Does It

To me, this is the most amazing part of the story of Jonah. God is determined to show His grace to Jonah no matter what. On the one hand, this reflects God's love for the Assyrians of Nineveh. On the other hand, God is also ensuring Jonah will fulfill the privilege of being His messenger, even though Jonah doesn't want the job anymore.

> *¹⁰For we are his workmanship, created in Christ Jesus for good works, which God prepared beforehand, that we should walk in them.*
> **—Ephesians 2:10**

God doesn't intend to let Jonah go too long wearing those ugly shoes we discussed in Chapter One. No matter how desperately Jonah's heart is set on comfortable, ugly shoes, God's plan has always been for Jonah to have beautiful feet. God's plan is to bring Jonah back to obedience, then use Jonah to call the people of Nineveh to Him.

In addition, we see a foreshadowing of what will ultimately happen with Nineveh: God also calls the sailors to turn to Jehovah! Thankfully for the prophet and the pagans—and for us–the Lord will spare no effort to display His mercy and to find and save those He has called.

How frustrating this must be for Satan! He must think

God is judging Jonah, these sailors are collateral damage, and Nineveh won't hear the good news of God's grace. The enemy thinks he has scored three wins—a dead prophet, a whole ship's crew, and an entire city—for the price of one disobedient soul. Nope! Satan's game plan will prove a colossal failure because God's grace cannot be impeded.

PERSONAL: WE CANNOT HIDE

Jonah convinces himself the best place to hide is in the belly of a ship on a voyage he doesn't need to take. *If you're hiding from what God has commanded you to do, don't get too comfortable, because no matter how well you think you've hidden, His grace is coming for you!*

Where We Hide

If you are trying to put some distance between you and God, you will probably pick a place where you'll feel comfortable. For example, Jonah finds a spot on the ship where he can get some peace and quiet, comfortably cut off from the world, without anyone to bother him. Like Jonah, most of us don't knowingly choose to hide in a storm. We seek a place where we can feel in control, even better if it's also a place where we can feel self-righteous. A refuge like that is perfectly conducive for hoarding grace and practicing selective obedience.

Conveniently, there are many such places like this in the world. We can hide from God in our work, our families, our leisure activities, and even our ministry activities. Careers are a popular hiding spot: "Oh, sorry, I'm too busy with work to serve, but one day I'll have more time for God!" Somehow "one day" always seems slow in coming.

Hiding from God and His word in our families is another neat trick. Yes, family should be a priority, but when we make it an excuse to avoid serving God and others in the ways the Lord requires, we turn family into a self-righteous hiding place. And I'll be the first to admit that during the Covid-19 pandemic, "Covid" became a ready-made excuse to avoid something God was calling me to do.

I think one of the best hiding places of all lies deep in the ship of the American church. Where better to hide from the Lord than in plain sight? The church has become a multi-billion-dollar industry replete with nooks and crannies to hide in, where sinfulness is bleached out and uncomfortable spiritual truths are habitually swept under the rug. Ensconced safely in our snug, Christian-themed hiding spots, we let the worship, the sermons, and the programs lull us into spiritual slumber. Then, fast asleep in our church cocoons, like Jonah fast asleep in the belly of the ship, we aren't disturbed by the stormy world around us.

This approach to our faith is a sinful, self-manipulative rationalization. It enables us to use the institution of the church to live cloaked in self-righteousness, but really, we're hiding from God and what He has called us to do, which is to serve the people caught outside in the storm.

Why We Hide

What is Jonah doing on that ship, anyway? What is his plan? Simply put, Jonah doesn't want to be fully obedient. He is hoarding grace from a group of people he hates more than he loves being near to God. When we are disobedient and hoard grace, we won't be able to be close to God; we'll find we need to isolate from Him, avoiding His word and ignoring His instruction. To maintain this distance from the Lord, we will find ways to hide, separating ourselves from His presence as Jonah does.

Surely there are things God has shown each of us through His word that we know we should address. How much of this revelation has gone unattended so we can remain comfortably set in our ways? If this is the case, it means we've found a hiding place. Perhaps when we encounter Jesus' teachings about purity, serving God, or the Great Commission to "make disciples of all nations" (Matthew 28:19), we acknowledge these commands but find excuses to drag our ugly feet when it comes to obeying them. Sometimes we seek refuge in seemingly less demanding scriptures, like the simple, familiar tale of a gigantic fish swallowing a stubborn prophet. If that's our thought process, we will be disappointed.

God Will Find Us

¹⁴...for anything that becomes visible is light. Therefore it says, "Awake, O sleeper, and arise from the dead, and Christ will shine on you."
—Ephesians 5:14

When it comes to God's pursuit of Jonah, even the steerage section of a cargo ship in the middle of the ocean isn't out of God's reach. The truth of God's omnipotence and omnipresence is all through Scripture, but these qualities of God aren't necessarily about the extent of His judgment. There is story after story in the Scriptures about the vast reach of God's sovereign grace. When we are children of God, He will come after us, He will find us, and He will do whatever He needs to do to bring us back to Him.

Take comfort in this promise: when we, as children of God, are hiding, He is going to do whatever it takes to draw us out of our places of isolation. That's not wrath or judgment; it's not God being angry. Rather, it's our loving Father chasing us with His gift of grace! This is what makes Him the Good Shepherd, relentlessly pursuing His wandering sheep. He will even use a terrible storm to save us from destruction if that's what it takes.

We started this chapter with an ominous, intimidating scripture from Jeremiah: "Am I a God at hand, declares the LORD, and not a God far away? Can a man hide himself in secret places so that I cannot see him? declares the LORD. Do I not fill heaven and earth? declares the LORD" (Jeremiah

23:23–24). The story of Jonah teaches us these words are a comforting truth, not a scary threat or cause for exasperation. We cannot hide from God, meaning we cannot hide from His grace!

> [11]*For thus says the Lord* GOD: *Behold, I, I myself will search for my sheep and will seek them out.*
> —*Ezekiel 34:11*

Pause here for a moment and reread the verse above to yourself. Read it a few times. Reflect on it and pray. Rejoice in the fact that if you are trying to hide from Him today in any way, He is coming after you. He will do whatever it takes to close the gap between your disobedience and His grace. I am so thankful God's children cannot hide from Him anywhere—aren't you?

Chapter Two Questions

Question: Does God's omnipresence intimidate you? Is our inability to evade His sight more frightening than comforting for you? Why or why not?

_____

_____

_____

_____

_____

_____

_____

_____

_____

_____

Question: What are some instances when your words or actions indicated you believed you were better than others? In what ways might your attitude toward other people have affected your willingness to be obedient to God?

_____

_____

_____

_____

_____

_____

_____

_____

_____

_____

Question: What places, responsibilities, hobbies, or relationships do you use to busy yourself and hide from God? In what ways are you avoiding His word or ignoring His instruction?

_____

_____

_____

_____

_____

_____

_____

_____

_____

_____

Action: Read and reflect on Ezekiel 34:11: "For thus says the Lord GOD: Behold, I, I myself will search for my sheep and will seek them out." In a journal, a notebook, or the notes section at the end of this chapter, write what God is communicating to you through this verse. Then spend some time (with worship music or on your own) giving thanks to

God and rejoicing that He will always be in eager pursuit of you.

Chapter Two Notes

_____

_____

_____

_____

_____

_____

_____

_____

_____

_____

_____

_____

_____

_____

_____

_____

Grace Is for Pagans

Have you ever been around a brand-new follower of Jesus, someone who just recently grasped the gospel? Their excitement and joy are hard to miss. I love their passion for more biblical knowledge! New believers ask so many questions. I think people in the beginning stages of their journey with God are often more teachable than those who have known Jesus for years. I love their hunger for fellowship and their desire to worship God and be obedient to His word.

Truth be told, it can be difficult for seasoned believers not to be a little envious of people who are new to faith. Maybe we feel shame for how complacency has crept into our own relationship with the Lord. We tend to become too familiar with the precious grace God has given us. We begin to take grace for granted and misplace our joy and excitement. We become self-centered, uninspired, and ungrateful. Oh, we still sing songs about grace and say "amen" to pithy quotes about it. We "like" the memes on social media about God's blessings. But our attitude toward God, His gifts, and His word can become ambivalent.

What causes this complacency? Why do we become comfortable with neglecting prayer and the word of God? When does worshiping in community become an obligation instead of a cherished opportunity? Deepening our relationship with the Lord should inspire passion, not apathy, yet somehow, we tend to lose that initial sense of wonder and amazement at His grace.

As we continue reading about Jonah in the storm, the contrast between the pagan sailors' attitude toward God and Jonah's attitude says much about the condition of the prophet's heart:

> [7]And they said to one another, "Come, let us cast lots, that we may know on whose account this evil has come upon us." So they cast lots, and the lot fell on Jonah. [8]Then they said to him, "Tell us on whose account this evil has come upon us. What is your occupation? And where do you come from? What is your country? And of what people are you?" [9]And he said to them, "I am a Hebrew, and I fear the LORD, the God of heaven, who made the sea and the dry land." [10]Then the men were exceedingly afraid and said to him, "What is this that you have done!" For the men knew that he was fleeing from the presence of the LORD, because he had told them.
>
> [11]Then they said to him, "What shall we do to you, that the sea may quiet down for us?" For the sea grew more and more tempestuous. [12]He said to them, "Pick me up and hurl me into the sea; then the sea will quiet down for you, for I know it is because of me that this great tempest has come upon you." [13]Nevertheless, the men rowed hard to get back to dry land, but they could not, for the sea grew more and

more tempestuous against them. [14]Therefore they called out to the LORD, "O LORD, let us not perish for this man's life, and lay not on us innocent blood, for you, O LORD, have done as it pleased you." [15]So they picked up Jonah and hurled him into the sea, and the sea ceased from its raging. [16]Then the men feared the LORD exceedingly, and they offered a sacrifice to the LORD and made vows.

—*Jonah 1:7–16*

HISTORICAL: IN THE SAME BOAT

Who's to Blame?

In this part of the story, Jonah and the sailors are in the same boat, literally and figuratively. Everyone is in desperate need of grace; everyone needs God to save him from the storm. However, I think we can learn a great deal from looking at the situation from the sailors' perspective.

To understand where the sailors are coming from, their conversation with Jonah, and their actions toward him, we need to recognize they are operating under a common pagan belief: when bad things happen, it means some god or gods are angry with someone. Based on that logic, if you want mercy, you must figure out which gods are angry, who made them angry and how, and how to appease the offended deities.

Caught in this fierce and sudden storm, these pagan mariners know some spiritual force beyond their comprehension is at work. In this crisis moment, they are desperate for spiritual enlightenment. They urgently want to know what god or gods have been angered, who has angered them, and what they, the sailors, can do about it. Running out of options, they cast lots, hoping whatever deity is causing the storm will reveal the culprit. God helps them out a little by letting the lot fall on Jonah. Now everyone knows the prophet is to blame!

Selfish Confession

Immediately, the sailors demand Jonah tell them who his God is and what Jonah has done to provoke his God to create this storm. Jonah promptly confesses everything: he is an Israelite prophet running from his God. But do not be impressed.

This confession is not an act of humility or repentance; rather, it's a selfish pity party. "Woe is me!" Jonah may as well be telling them. "If you want to save yourselves, all you must do is toss me into the sea and let me drown. Since God has given me the worst assignment a poor prophet like me could imagine, you may as well let me drown in the sea."

But God doesn't want Jonah to drown. All Jonah needs to tell the sailors is to turn the ship around and take him back so he can go to Nineveh, like he was supposed to do in the first place. Far from repentant, Jonah is so stubborn he prefers a watery grave to delivering God's message to the Assyrians. Even in the storm, Jonah remains committed to his grace-hoarding ways, but God isn't going to let Jonah off the hook. He still wants His prophet to preach.

Teachable Pagans

Hesitant to throw Jonah overboard, the sailors keep fighting to get back to shore. These pagan sailors care more about the prophet than the prophet cares about them, which shows the Lord is already at work in their hearts. But the harder they try to save Jonah, the worse the storm gets. Finally, this pagan crew cries out to Jonah's God for mercy because they know He is real. With the unusual storm, the lot falling on Jonah, and the prophet's confession, how can they not believe in Him?

In this moment, the sailors want to be right with God, but they don't know how. Conveniently enough, they have a prophet of God on board, so they ask him. "The storm is getting worse!" we can imagine them exclaiming. "Tell us, Jonah, what do we need to do to appease your God? Teach us about your God!" Don't breeze past this moment, because it is miraculous: in a crisis, these men abandon all the pagan gods they have worshiped their entire lives to seek merciful intervention from Jehovah. But when they turn to this rebellious, bigoted, selfish prophet for wisdom about God, Jonah refuses to preach!

Finally, the sailors relent, reluctantly following Jonah's advice and throwing him into the sea. That's when the most inspiring part of this story takes place. On the spot, the sailors become worshipers of God: "Then the men feared the LORD exceedingly, and they offered a sacrifice to the LORD and made vows" (Jonah 1:16). At this point, the pagan sailors are more in tune with God than the wise, old, experienced prophet is!

SPIRITUAL: GRACE DESPITE ALL

As the storm rages around them, it is impossible for the sailors or Jonah to comprehend the full scope of what God is doing in these moments. All these poor pagan sailors know is someone's god is angry and they are caught in the crossfire.

Understandably, the sailors don't know how to come to God like nice, obedient Jews. Instead, they come to Him as pagans, using the pagan ritual of casting lots. Yet God, in His grace, chooses to reveal spiritual truth through that pagan ritual! Do we, as believers, have a problem with that? I'm guessing Jonah probably did.

Grace Despite Ignorance

The idea of speaking to pagan sailors through the casting of lots may further offend Jonah's sensitive soul, but it isn't beyond God. In fact, God speaking truth in pagan places is another example of His graciousness and mercy. With the light of His truth, He breaks down pagan barriers of darkness erected by the enemy in the hearts of men!

In other words, God loves those pagan sailors so much He doesn't allow pagan ignorance to hinder grace. Though God's truth does not change, He can reveal truth in any circumstance. He does it for those sailors, as He continues to do it in our lives and our world today.

Grace Despite Jonah

Based on what we know of Jonah's character and behavior up to this point, how do you think he views these sailors when he first gets on the ship? It seems he has no interest in interacting with them. Even in his own pitiful spiritual state, Jonah looks down on these sailors. As far as he's concerned, he is better than them, which means the last thing on his mind is teaching a shipload of pagans about Jehovah! After all, Jonah is mired in a full-blown personal crisis, wallowing in victim mode. He would rather drown than teach the sailors or preach in Nineveh.

Jonah, in his pride, prefers disobedience, even to the point of death, but God is going to use him anyway. God uses the circumstances of Jonah's arrogant, selfish disobedience to call the sailors to faith and worship of the one true God. Despite the prophet's rebellious attitude, the grace God has reserved for the pagan sailors will not be impeded!

PERSONAL: BORED WITH GRACE?

In this part of the story, the two reactions to God's presence could not be more different. Why would pagans respond with greater faith and obedience than a prophet of the Lord? This speaks to a bigger question: *Why are unbelievers often more teachable than Christians?*

Celebrating Grace

The sailors wake up that morning to do what they always do. They have no plan for or intention of seeking God. However, by day's end, they are filled with wonder, awe, gratitude, and joy. They become worshipers of Jehovah! No doubt, their experience is a powerful story they will retell to their families and to fellow sailors for years to come. It's the great story of their time: they faced certain death but ended up being transformed by God's grace.

If this story were to happen today, I wouldn't be able to get enough of hearing them talk about how God had saved them! I would follow them on Twitter, "friend" them on Facebook, and subscribe to their podcast. For the sailors, it is surely the best day of their lives.

Ironically, for Jonah, it is the low point of his life. How can that be? How can this incredible moment of pagan sailors converting to worshipers of God not be something to celebrate, especially for a prophet? Somehow Jonah has come to a place where pagan sailors are more excited about the things of God than he is.

Neglecting Grace

We may not be quick to recognize this, but often unbelievers are more excited about grace than we are. Jonah isn't the first or the last believer to grow bored with grace. Maybe you have known Jesus for a long time but can't seem to find much joy in your relationship with Him anymore. When this happens, we become more like Jonah than the sailors, choosing the secluded isolation of self-pity over the joys of grace.

Many people who attend church for years don't celebrate grace with joy or enthusiasm anymore; instead, they neglect it. They neglect fellowship with other believers; they neglect service and ministry. They let prayer slide and allow God's word to fall by the wayside. We can easily become so wrapped up in our own lives, our own little world, we're afraid to interact with anyone outside of it. In these cases, we're far more interested in the personal benefits of grace than how grace may be at work outside the church. As a result, we spend more effort avoiding pagans than we do seeking opportunities to teach them. Oh, we'll talk about outreach and budget for missions, and we'll dutifully applaud the missionaries. But we don't really do much outreach ourselves. Like Jonah, we just aren't feeling it. We tell ourselves we've got more than enough problems of our own already.

As a result, people inside the church can become disconnected from grace and from God's power. This makes us no better than the pagans! In fact, it makes us worse, because we know the truth and choose to ignore it.

Reunited with Grace

I wonder if Jonah ever learned what happened to those sailors after they threw him into the sea. When he looked back on that moment of crisis and thought about the men who were caught in the storm with him, what ran through his mind? At the time, he certainly wasn't interested in the ship's crew, because all he could think about was his own trouble.

Now, who would you rather be in this story, Jonah or the sailors? Whose response to God in the storm seems more satisfying?

The psalmist recognizes the deep joy found in sinners turning to the Lord:

> [12]*Restore to me the joy of your salvation, and uphold me with a willing spirit. [13]Then I will teach transgressors your ways, and sinners will return to you.*
> —*Psalm 51:12–13*

The reality of God's grace in action is never boring. In fact, Scripture testifies to this reality. We should always marvel at God's love and mercies, which are new, fresh, and exciting every day!

> [22]*The steadfast love of the LORD never ceases; his mercies never come to an end; [23]they are new every morning; great is your faithfulness.*
> —*Lamentations 3:22–23*

If God's love and mercies are new every morning, why are we—who may have known the Lord for years—cold to spiritual truths? Why are we more like Jonah than the sailors? Simply put, we've fallen into the trap of taking God's grace for granted. Wouldn't you love to go back to the moment when God found you, as He found those pagan sailors? Have you lost your appreciation for God's grace? You must become like the sailors, remembering how desperately you need Him. Grace can seem boring only if we forget how much we need it! That is what happens with Jonah, which explains how he can be so callous toward the sailors and the people of Nineveh.

Come to the Father, confessing your boredom with His grace. Ask Him to make mercy new again for you and remind you of His grace toward pagans. Pray for renewed passion in your attitude toward Him and compassion toward others. Ask the Lord to give you the tender heart of a pagan sailor hearing the gospel for the first time, so you don't forget you need it as much as anyone else does!

Chapter Three Questions

Question: How do you feel when you witness a new believer's enthusiasm for God? Does it remind you of the beginning of your walk with Him? How does your current relationship with God compare to when it first began? Have you settled into complacency? What choices or patterns have led to this complacency? What steps can you take to reignite your enthusiastic commitment to Christ?

_____

_____

_____

_____

_____

_____

_____

_____

_____

_____

_____

Question: How and when did God reveal Himself to you? What does this remind you about God's grace? What does it mean for those around you who may seem beyond God's reach? How does this impact how you see them?

_____

_____

_____

_____

_____

_____

_____

_____

_____

Question: Are you regularly neglecting grace, fellowship with other believers, or service and ministry? What has become a higher priority in your life than your relationship with God? What do you need to do to restore your gratitude for God's grace?

_____

_____

_____

_____

_____

_____

_____

_____

_____

Action: Spend some time in prayer, confessing your boredom with God's grace. Pray for the Holy Spirit to renew your passion for God's grace toward you and compassion toward others.

Chapter Three Notes

_____

_____

_____

_____

_____

_____

_____

_____

_____

_____

_____

_____

_____

_____

_____

_____

Real Confession

Have you ever confessed without really meaning it? I'm talking about a confession without real remorse or repentance, like "Yeah, I flipped that guy off at the red light, and I'm glad I did. He deserved it!"

What about a humble brag disguised as a confession? "Sorry I cussed you out. I just tend to tell it like it is."

Then there's false self-deprecation: "Yeah, best watch out, I have a little bit of an anger problem."

Have you ever used a confession to drum up pity or compassion, to manipulate people into feeling sorry for you? "I made some bad choices, and now I'm suffering the consequences." You're just inviting people to feel bad for you.

What about confession combined with promises we don't intend to keep? "I'm so sorry. Just give me one more chance!" Those confessions can seem genuine, but really, they are fertile ground for self-deception and false spirituality.

Let's be honest: we've all offered insincere confessions,

without repentance or brokenness. These false confessions are particularly self-destructive and indicate a deeper spiritual problem.

However, there are moments of real confession. Have you ever been truly repentant, teachable, humble, and broken? Can you remember the last time you experienced the cathartic, healing power of sincere confession? We must be able to tell the difference between real and false confession to ensure we aren't deceiving ourselves. In making this distinction, we can learn a great deal from Jonah:

> *[17]And the LORD appointed a great fish to swallow up Jonah. And Jonah was in the belly of the fish three days and three nights. [1]Then Jonah prayed to the LORD his God from the belly of the fish, [2]saying, "I called out to the LORD, out of my distress, and he answered me; out of the belly of Sheol I cried, and you heard my voice. [3]For you cast me into the deep, into the heart of the seas, and the flood surrounded me; all your waves and your billows passed over me. [4]Then I said, 'I am driven away from your sight; yet I shall again look upon your holy temple.' [5]The waters closed in over me to take my life; the deep surrounded me; weeds were wrapped about my head [6]at the roots of the mountains. I went down to the land whose bars closed upon me forever; yet you brought up my life from the pit, O LORD my God. [7]When my life was fainting away, I remembered the LORD, and my prayer came to you, into your holy temple. [8]Those who pay regard to vain idols forsake their hope of steadfast love. [9]But I with the voice of thanksgiving will sacrifice to you; what I have vowed I will pay. Salvation belongs to the LORD!" [10]And the LORD spoke to the fish, and it vomited Jonah out upon the dry land.*
>
> **—Jonah 1:17–2:10**

HISTORICAL: JONAH'S BEST MOMENT

Imagine what Jonah is thinking as the sailors throw him overboard. Imagine what he is feeling as he splashes into the billowing waves. Suddenly, the ugly reality of the circumstances surrounding his refusal to go to Nineveh are laid bare before him. He chose to run in the opposite direction, to Tarshish, instead of traveling to Nineveh as God instructed. He chose to tell the sailors to throw him overboard instead of simply turning the boat around. And now this selfish, arrogant, bigoted, self-loathing, rebellious prophet is about to drown in a foreign sea, never to be heard from again.

Maybe King Jeroboam will look around one day and ask, "Where's that Jonah guy? I could use a good pick-me-up prophecy today. Has anyone seen him?" And no one will know where the prophet has disappeared to.

Overwhelmed with sheer terror as he struggles for breath, Jonah finally realizes all his kvetching about Nineveh is utterly foolish. Then, suddenly, with perfect timing, a God-appointed whale ("great fish") swallows him. For the next three days, Jonah will be stuck in this strange, organic life raft.

Three Days in a Big Fish

Here, in the whale's belly, Jonah can no longer run. Because the stubborn prophet keeps resisting God's call, the Lord finally grabs Jonah's undivided attention for three days. Keep in mind this isn't a cruise ship; it's the dark, clammy, smelly interior of a gigantic fish. On top of the odor, imagine the pressure changes every time the whale dives deeper or swims closer to the surface. I would guess it's about as close to hell on earth as anyone can get.

God has tolerated quite a bit from Jonah to bring him to a place of real confession, and now, inside a fish, He accomplishes His purpose. At this point, Jonah has lost all control over his circumstances. Even if he wants to admit he is wrong and set course immediately for Nineveh, there is no longer a ship or crew at his disposal. Here, in the worst moment of Jonah's life, the full-on pity party finally ends, and something begins to change in his heart.

Though Jonah has become teachable, notice he doesn't pray his confession right after the whale swallows him, but days later. It would be fascinating to know the details of how his heart and mind progress to confession. The important thing, however, is God's grace brings him to it.

Jonah's Prayer

Jonah's prayer is rich, deep, and meaningful, everything we might expect in a real confession. In the space of a few sentences, the prophet recognizes his sin, confesses it, and expresses his desire for restoration with God. He wants to enjoy the Lord's presence again, serving Him and returning to His temple.

In a further sign of his sincere change of heart, Jonah expresses his gratitude to God for rescuing him from the sea, even though this rescue comes in the form of a big fish's belly. Amid the foul, miserable, frightening consequences of his sin, Jonah is humbled to the point where he can see the whale as his salvation.

SPIRITUAL: SECOND CONFESSION

Of course, we know this isn't Jonah's first confession. Remember what he tells the pagan mariners in chapter 1:

> ¹²He said to them, "Pick me up and hurl me into the sea; then the sea will quiet down for you, for I know it is because of me that this great tempest has come upon you."
> —Jonah 1:12

If we compare Jonah's two confessions, one to men and the other to the Lord, we can see just how different they are.

Confession to Men

In Chapter Three, we saw how Jonah's first confession isn't sincere. He intends it to be heard by men alone, which means it is directed to the wrong audience. Also, he intends the confession to elicit sympathy, with no humility or desire for repentance. That confession has all the wrong motives.

But Jonah's first confession accomplishes its intended purpose. Jonah manipulates the sailors to the point of putting their own lives at risk as they struggle through the storm. If Jonah really cared about them and honestly thought the only solution was to put him in the sea, he could have jumped overboard by himself. Instead, he puts the decision on the sailors, which seems perverse, but let's admit we are all capable of the same thing. We have all manipulated people into making a choice we should have made ourselves.

All Jonah cares about at this point is getting his way and getting people to feel pity for his condition. He doesn't yet believe he deserves the consequences of the storm, so he is not interested in repentance. Consumed with self-pity, Jonah doesn't really acknowledge his failure; rather, he complains God is singling him out unfairly.

Confession to God

Jonah's second confession is different. After three days in the belly of this whale, something changes. This new confession isn't for men's ears. There are no people to hear him. With no one to manipulate and nowhere to hide, his confession is for God's ears alone, an audience of one. God brings Jonah to circumstances in which the prophet has no choice but to rely on Him alone.

This second confession comprises past (e.g., "For you cast me into the deep"), present ("I am driven away from your sight"), and future ("I with the voice of thanksgiving will sacrifice to you") elements. Taken all together, Jonah's words reflect a new posture of humility and a recognition that his overwhelming circumstances are of his own making. When he is "fainting away," he doesn't blame the Lord or the Ninevites, but instead "remember[s] the LORD" and expresses gratitude for how God "brought up [his] life from the pit." Jonah himself has been the problem, and he is finally willing to admit as much. After Jonah "remember[s] the LORD," taking responsibility for and committing to repent of his disobedient ways, he then expresses a desire to be restored to a position of serving God "with the voice of thanksgiving."

Only God can lead Jonah's heart to this place of repentance and restoration, which tells us this second confession is the Lord's work, not Jonah's human effort. By the grace of God, the prophet finally offers God a real confession meant for His ears only.

Results of Confession

> ³¹For the Lord will not cast off forever, ³²but, though he cause grief, he will have compassion according to the abundance of his steadfast love....
> **—Lamentations 3:31–32**

This is how God works in the hearts and lives of those He loves, making full use of circumstances—even those of our own making—to create a miraculous, heavenly moment! As a result of Jonah's confession, God gives him a chance to fulfill his promised repentance and preach to the Ninevites. The prophet's heavenly confession after three days moves God to action, and the whale spits Jonah out.

PERSONAL: HEAVENLY CONFESSION

[10]For godly grief produces a repentance that leads to salvation without regret, whereas worldly grief produces death.
—2 Corinthians 7:10

Within this verse, we clearly see there are two types of confession: heavenly and earthly. *The human heart is wholly incapable of sincere, heavenly confession—until our heavenly Dad intervenes.*

Earthly Confession

Can a confession be sinful? Well, we've seen how Jonah's first confession is an arrogant expression of selfishness, indulgence in self-pity, and manipulation. How often have we fallen into this trap of confessing with sinful motives, inspired by self-pity? Instead of being a way to get right with God, such confession serves our own selfish interests.

Earthly confession is an expression of having more concern for yourself than for those impacted by your sinfulness. It can be a passive-aggressive tool to manipulate others by attracting sympathy or sacrifice for your benefit. It can take the form of a brag clothed in false humility, as mentioned at the beginning of this chapter. "I am so competitive on the basketball court; I just hate losing," we might confess. Or, better yet, "Pray for me—I am really struggling with materialism with all this money I am making."

Earthly confession also has a way of leaving out the worst details so we can hide our shame and avoid taking full responsibility. Kids learn to do this to avoid getting into too much trouble, but adults are equally capable (and have had a lot more practice). This earthly confession is an attempt to ease our guilt and shame so we can sleep at night while skipping that annoying step of repentance. Earthly confession always has the goal of minimizing consequences, begging for mercy we don't deserve. I don't mean we desire mercy leading to forgiveness. I mean we want a "God, get me out of this jam!" variety of mercy that rescues us from the consequences of our sin.

Heavenly Confession

When you experience a heavenly confession, you will know the difference immediately. Heavenly confession, inspired by the work of the Holy Spirit, contains none of those toxic qualities I described above.

After studying Jonah's heavenly confession, I was reminded of another famous confession in the Bible, in Psalm 51, which begins:

[1]Have mercy on me, O God, according to your steadfast love; according to your abundant mercy blot out my transgressions. [2]Wash me thoroughly from my iniquity, and cleanse me from my sin!

—Psalm 51:1–2

Comparing Jonah's confession with David's confession of adultery (with Bathsheba) and murder (of her husband, Uriah), we can develop a more detailed anatomy of a heavenly confession. These two biblical examples give us a clearer idea of what to look for so we can know when our confession is born of the Lord, not of our human nature:

Heavenly confession begins with heavenly intervention. It's not something we can generate on our own.

Heavenly confession can't be managed, manipulated, or constructed by human effort or intelligence.

Heavenly confession is often "off schedule." It's not a part of our initial plan for managing our sin.

Heavenly confession is the inevitable result of God's Spirit calling His children to mercy and repentance.

Heavenly confession is the result of God finding a wandering heart and bringing it into line with His sovereign plan.

Heavenly confession starts with understanding the filth of our sinfulness. Then it pleads for forgiveness!

Heavenly confession, born of brokenness and humility, doesn't care about consequences, only restoration.

Heavenly confession teaches us to embrace the consequences that brought us to the point of brokenness.

As David said:

⁸Let me hear joy and gladness; let the bones that you have broken rejoice.

—Psalm 51:8

Heavenly confession sees those consequences as grace, not judgment. The lessons we learn from consequences become precious spiritual moments we never forget. Have you had moments when God used circumstances to restore you to what He has called you to be?

Heavenly confession compels you to run to the comfort of the cross instead of the comfort offered by the world.

Heavenly confession creates a bond with others who have experienced this same type of miraculous intervention. Don't be fooled: persistent isolation from God's people is a strong indicator that heavenly confession is absent. God forms a supernatural connection between those of us who have shared the experience of heavenly confession. We develop a desire to walk the same path together, as sinners who are celebrating mercy and restoration through the work of Christ. Through corporate worship, corporate service, and even corporate repentance, we are meant to celebrate that restoration together!

Heavenly confession isn't just remembering the shame of past failures. Rather, it goes beyond shame to hope in future restoration. If we ever wonder why we don't have much to say to others about Jesus, it may be because heavenly confession is missing from our relationship with Him.

¹²Restore to me the joy of your salvation, and uphold me with a willing spirit. ¹³Then I will teach transgressors your ways, and sinners will return to you.

—Psalm 51:12–13

Heavenly confession restores the joy of that first day we embraced the gospel and inspires us to teach others. The murderous adulterer David experienced this restoration of joy in the Lord, as did rebellious, self-centered Jonah, and heavenly confession will accomplish the same thing in your heart!

Heavenly confession is a surreal moment only a redeemed heart can experience and understand. It is a cherished preview of the day we will cease struggling with sin and exist in perfect fellowship with Jesus. In a moment of real confession, the disgusting, smelly stomach of a gigantic fish can become the sweetest place on earth.

Are you in a whale's belly of your own making today, suffering the consequences of your own sinfulness? Take heart, child of God, because you could be on the verge of one of the most precious, pivotal moments of your life! If you have never experienced a supernatural, heavenly confession, now would be the perfect time.

Chapter Four Questions

Question: Describe ways you have used confession as something other than a pathway to genuine repentance. Have you ever used it to brag, justify your behavior, drum up pity or compassion, or manipulate others into feeling sorry for you? Have you ever confessed while making empty promises? How does this type of confession keep you from true transformation?

_____

_____

_____

_____

_____

_____

_____

_____

_____

_____

_____

_____

Question: Have you ever been truly repentant, teachable, humble, and broken? Can you remember the last time you experienced the cathartic, healing power of sincere, heavenly confession? What does this reveal to you about the impact of authentic confession?

_____

_____

_____

_____

_____

_____

_____

_____

_____

_____

_____

Question: Are you in a whale's belly of your own making today, suffering the consequences of your own sinfulness? What lead you to this place? What do you think God is attempting to communicate to you through these consequences?

_____

_____

_____

_____

_____

_____

_____

_____

_____

_____

_____

Action: Review the list of descriptors of heavenly confession. Is there anything you currently need to confess and pursue repentance for? Spend some time in prayer over the course of a day, week, or month (as long as it takes!), inviting God to bring your heart to a place of genuine, heavenly confession and repentance.

Chapter Four Notes

God's Judgment

If I tell you this chapter is about fearing God and God's judgment of sinners, what is your first thought? How do you feel about the topics of hell and God's judgment? Back in my Southern Baptist days, we called sermons like that "hellfire and brimstone." Those sermons have become rare.

Today, the wrath of God is one of the most neglected doctrines in sermons and books. Some pastors and writers are afraid to mention it. They put significant effort into keeping God's wrath out of their messages, which requires them to avoid many passages about hell and judgment.

What are we to believe about fearing God? How should followers of Jesus manage this important part of the gospel? Can God be feared, yet loved and worshiped at the same time? Can our God really be so vindictive He threatens to judge sinners?

When sharing the love of Jesus and the gospel, should we shy away from talking about judgment? Is it manipulation to preach it, as if we're scaring people into repentance? Should we focus only on love, mercy, and forgiveness?

This chapter's critical swimming lesson is how *fear of the Lord is one of the keys to a life of true repentance and worship.*

> [1]Then the word of the LORD came to Jonah the second time, saying, [2]"Arise, go to Nineveh, that great city, and call out against it the message that I tell you." [3]So Jonah arose and went to Nineveh, according to the word of the LORD. Now Nineveh was an exceedingly great city, three days' journey in breadth. [4]Jonah began to go into the city, going a day's journey. And he called out, "Yet forty days, and Nineveh shall be overthrown!" [5]And the people of Nineveh believed God. They called for a fast and put on sackcloth, from the greatest of them to the least of them.
>
> [6]The word reached the king of Nineveh, and he arose from his throne, removed his robe, covered himself with sackcloth, and sat in ashes. [7]And he issued a proclamation and published through Nineveh, "By the decree of the king and his nobles: Let neither man nor beast, herd nor flock, taste anything. Let them not feed or drink water, [8]but let man and beast be covered with sackcloth, and let them call out mightily to God. Let everyone turn from his evil way and from the violence that is in his hands. [9]Who knows? God may turn and relent and turn from his fierce anger, so that we may not perish."
>
> [10]When God saw what they did, how they turned from their evil way, God relented of the disaster that he had said he would do to them, and he did not do it.
>
> **—Jonah 3:1–10**

HISTORICAL: PREACHING JUDGMENT

Jonah's miraculous heavenly confession spawns immediate repentance. Finally, he heads straight to the Assyrians in Nineveh!

Repentance for Miles

Don't be fooled by how short the passage about Jonah's ministry in Nineveh is. It likely takes months, even a year. It's not a weeklong foreign mission trip like we do in churches today, with vacation elements mixed in. Jonah is there for a while, preaching about judgment and repentance. In his day, Nineveh is so massive, it takes three days to travel from one end to the other (Jonah 3:3). In other words, Jonah's repentance isn't convenient or cost-free. It's the exact opposite! It totally disrupts his current life plans.

Enjoyable Repentance?

However, even in his repentance, I imagine Jonah likely enjoys warning pagans about God's plan to judge them if they don't repent. Imagine his passion in delivering sermons of imminent judgment on the Assyrians. I bet Jonah is motivated, articulate, and clear, not holding anything back. He is preaching a message about God's wrath to people he still doesn't really like. He is preaching judgment and the command to repent, just as God told him to do. Certainly, when all is said and done, Jonah anticipates the Ninevites will not repent, and God will judge Israel's enemies.

Though Jonah has recently experienced the lengths God will go to in order to ensure those He has called to repentance hear His voice, I'm sure Jonah is optimistic that the results will still be what he wants in Nineveh. It's the best of both worlds! Jonah is being obedient, *and* he believes he is preaching a message that will produce results in harmony with his patriotic political worldview—that God will judge the enemies of Israel.

Unexpected Results

Then something unexpected happens: "the people of Nineveh believed God" (Jonah 3:5). They join Jonah in repentance! This goes much further than the Ninevites choosing to believe in God. Many Christians today are willing to take the step of believing but then offer up repentance that is symbolic at best. The Ninevites' repentance isn't symbolic or superficial. It is a transformation much deeper than simply believing in God.

Fear of God's judgment inspires the Ninevites to ask forgiveness, personally and corporately. This repentance isn't limited to certain segments of society or groups of people. Everyone repents, even the king himself, and their actions validate their sincerity. They change who they worship, how they worship, and how they dress. Their transformation goes so deep it alters their culture and core values for the next several generations.

SPIRITUAL: FEAR AND WISDOM

Jonah is surprised, in a bad way, by the Ninevites' repentance, but God certainly isn't.

Part of the Plan

It's logical to assume Jonah is the central focus of the book named after him, but he isn't. The book of Jonah is about God's love for a pagan nation. God's love for Nineveh is what motivates His patience with the prophet in the first place. God always intends for Nineveh to believe and repent, just as He intends for Jonah to repent and preach to them. God isn't going to allow Jonah's disobedience to derail His plan to bring Nineveh to repentance. Instead, God will do whatever it takes to get Jonah to Nineveh to preach the gospel and open the door for God to save the Ninevites.

God of Judgment

"God is a God of love!" This is a popular assertion by many people, both Christians and non-Christians. Of course, it's true, but there are sides to God's character besides love—or, at least, besides the feel-good kind of love people usually mean when they say things like that. The Ninevites' repentance isn't the result of a watered-down, pagan-friendly message about kindness, universal salvation, and the like. They repent because of an unfiltered message about facing the wrath of God if they fail to believe and repent.

You might ask: Why would God do that? It seems so mean! Why doesn't God bring Nineveh to repentance with love? Why doesn't He tell Jonah to put on a well-produced worship concert or a seminar featuring healings and outpourings of compassion? Why doesn't God show the Ninevites He is real through generous miracles and glorious signs? Well, luckily for us, Jesus explains:

> ²⁹*When the crowds were increasing, he [Jesus] began to say, "This generation is an evil generation. It seeks for a sign, but no sign will be given to it except the sign of Jonah. ³⁰For as Jonah became a sign to the people of Nineveh, so will the Son of Man be to this generation. … ³²The men of Nineveh will rise up at the judgment with this generation and condemn it, for they repented at the preaching of Jonah, and behold, something greater than Jonah is here.*
> —*Luke 11:29–30, 32*

Jesus' generation sees great miracles and expressions of Christ's love, yet most still don't believe. They witness Jesus providing healings, feedings, compassion for the lowly, and even resurrection of dead relatives. You would think after all this, many more would put their faith in Jesus, but they don't. Miracles are not enough to convince them.

Notice how Jesus compares Himself to Jonah. Merciful, loving, miracle-working, compassionate Jesus is also the Jesus who condemns sin and warns about judgment, demanding repentance.

The Beginning of Wisdom

God uses Jonah's warnings of judgment to bring a necessary fear of God to the Assyrians of Nineveh, leading them to repent. Indeed, there is a side to God to be feared. How do you feel about the fact that God is to be feared? There are dozens of scriptures throughout the Bible about fearing God's wrath being the first step of faith:

> *⁷The fear of the LORD is the beginning of knowledge; fools despise wisdom and instruction.*
>
> **—Proverbs 1:7**

> *¹⁰The fear of the LORD is the beginning of wisdom, and the knowledge of the Holy One is insight.*
>
> **—Proverbs 9:10**

> *²⁷The fear of the LORD is a fountain of life, that one may turn away from the snares of death.*
>
> **—Proverbs 14:27**

> *²³The fear of the LORD leads to life, and whoever has it rests satisfied; he will not be visited by harm.*
>
> **—Proverbs 19:23**

Miracles and love represent only a partial picture of the gospel. Without fear, there is no wisdom; without wisdom, there is no faith; without faith, there is no salvation. In fact, preaching the gospel without warning about judgment hides the genuine cost of mercy and grace! But teaching people the necessity of fearing God isn't a popular message today.

PERSONAL: THE FEAR OF THE LORD

Let's get to the question at the heart of this subject: Should warnings about God's judgment be a part of our proclamation of the gospel?

> *22And have mercy on those who doubt; 23save others by snatching them out of the fire; to others show mercy with fear, hating even the garment stained by the flesh.*
> **—Jude 1:22–23**

Most people are willing to identify with a merciful and gracious God, but not with a God of judgment and wrath. We must learn to embrace the truth that there is legitimate fear and terror to be had outside of Christ. Jesus says judgment and wrath will fall on those who don't embrace the gospel. Sorry, but that's what our Lord says!

Many churches claim to love God and His truth but avoid what the Bible declares about fear being the beginning of wisdom. Ironically, they fear the world's rejection more than they fear God's judgment, which leads them to try to quarantine the judgment aspect of God's word. But avoiding biblical warnings of God's judgment indicates you want God to work on your terms, not His! It reveals an attitude that will justify, tolerate, and even embrace the sugarcoating or flat-out rejection of inconvenient aspects of the truth. When people do this, they are appointing themselves final judges over which words of Jesus are palatable and which should be ignored.

Here's the problem with that mindset: without understanding the fear of God's judgment, no one can understand the gift of faith. Teachings about God's mercy and grace lose their value if we deny the reality of His judgment.

> [10]For we must all appear before the judgment seat of Christ, so that each one may receive what is due for what he has done in the body, whether good or evil.
>
> [11]Therefore, knowing the fear of the Lord, we persuade others. But what we are is known to God, and I hope it is known also to your conscience.
> **—2 Corinthians 5:10–11**

People tend to want to play around the edges of faith. Some believe there's a God, and they may also believe Jesus died on the cross and rose again, yet they stop short of true repentance. Why? Because they don't really fear God's judgment.

Are you living in denial of the undeniable reality that judgment of sin is a part of the gospel message, as Jesus Himself has declared? Are you still waiting for one more piece to fall into place to persuade you that full, sincere repentance is worth the trouble? What more does God need to do for you to surrender completely to the gospel?

Maybe you want to see a miracle. Perhaps you are waiting

to stumble upon one final, overwhelmingly convincing piece of tangible, scientific, or archeological proof. Maybe you're holding out for some mountaintop worship experience or for the Lord to appear to you in a dream or vision. What is it going to take?

Of course, powerful experiences like those can encourage and strengthen our faith. They are awesome! But Scripture says those things don't give us spiritual wisdom. *The fear of the Lord is what brings us wisdom.* Once we understand the fear of the Lord, something miraculous happens: we no longer need to fear God, because we can finally understand the depth and power of His love for us. We now have the wisdom necessary to appreciate fully those other signs and wonders.

> [18]There is no fear in love, but perfect love casts out fear. For fear has to do with punishment, and whoever fears has not been perfected in love.
> **—1 John 4:18**

As we have read in God's word, fear is the beginning of understanding the gospel. Fear of the Lord is the most basic, fundamental swimming lesson you can learn from the book of Jonah. The fear of the Lord is what instills wisdom within our hearts regarding how and why God hates and punishes sin. It brings us to a posture of spiritual humility, helping us understand God is judge and we deserve His judgment. This fear of God's judgment gives birth to the precious gift of desperation, which leads to faith and the perfect love of Jesus, which casts out all fear of punishment. In this respect, the fear of the Lord is a lifesaving revelation!

In other words, fear of the Lord is the first, most important catalyst for full, true repentance and transformation. It teaches us just how much God loves His chosen, even to the point of being willing to endure the cross. Fear of the Lord is the grace of God warning you, calling you to safety from His judgment into His perfect love. The fear of the Lord enables us to understand how precious and costly grace, mercy, and forgiveness through the cross really are. This fear is what can bring us to a place of true joy, gratitude, and worship.

So, I ask you again: What are you waiting for? Will you confess God's right to judge sin, specifically *your* sin? Are you ready to confess His majesty, holiness, and power? Are you ready to acknowledge His right to judgment and wrath? That's where true spiritual wisdom begins! Only then will you fully comprehend the riches of God's mercy and grace. Only then will you understand why you need true, full repentance.

Otherwise, your spirituality is nothing more than a quest for momentary distractions from what you truly deserve. Until you experience fear of the Lord leading to repentance, you won't experience the peace and safety of the arms of a loving Father. Until then, you have no way to accept or understand the perfect love of Jesus.

Chapter Five Questions

Question: What are your thoughts and feelings in response to the mention of God's wrath and judgment of sinners? How do you reconcile that doctrine with the doctrine of a loving God?

_____

_____

_____

_____

_____

_____

_____

_____

_____

_____

Question: Are there any ways in which your political and/or ethnocentric worldview hinder you from seeing people (in your city, in your country, or around the world) from God's perspective? How does this impact your ability to extend His love and grace to them? What role does the message of God's judgment play in your ability to reach others?

_____

_____

_____

_____

_____

_____

_____

_____

_____

_____

Question: How do you feel about the fact God is to be feared? Why do you think God doesn't use only feel-good experiences, such as miracles and outpouring of love, to bring people to repentance? Do you avoid sharing the full picture of God's salvation message when you share Christ with others? Why or why not?

_____

_____

_____

_____

_____

_____

_____

_____

_____

_____

Action: In a notebook or journal, spend time writing a prayer inviting God to show you the full picture of who He is: His wrath and His grace. Ask God to humble you and show you the ways in which your own sins are deserving of His wrath.

Chapter Five Notes

_____

_____

_____

_____

_____

_____

_____

_____

_____

_____

_____

_____

_____

_____

_____

_____

_____

Mad at God

I had a friend—whom I had not heard from in several years—reach out to me, asking if he could borrow fifty dollars. I figured, *"No big deal. I am super-generous!"* Also, I am very modern and hip, so I told him I would send him fifty dollars through Venmo. I anticipated my friend would be grateful. I waited for the gracious reply. Instead, my long-lost friend insisted I send the fifty dollars through another service, called Cash App. "I don't have Cash App," I replied. "I don't use Cash App."

He got frustrated. "Joe, can you just open a Cash App account? It's what I use. It's easier for me that way."

"Nah," I responded, "you open a Venmo account, and I will send you the money."

My friend's response was bizarre: "Never mind, just forget it. I will go hungry."

I thought to myself, *"Okay, good talk!"*

Unexpectedly, someone who hadn't spoken to me in years

asked for money and then got frustrated because I wouldn't help him on his terms. I was thinking to myself, *"Where's the gratitude, dude?"*

Many Christians have the same bizarre approach to God. When we discover God's plan does not fit ours, we get frustrated. How can people who have received the riches of God's mercy, love, and grace ever be frustrated with Him? But often, without realizing it, we do get frustrated with God and how He chooses to work.

Have you ever been angry at God? Have you ever been frustrated with how the Lord does things? Have you ever been in that place in your relationship with Him? We all need to learn how to spot this pattern in our hearts.

We might say, "Oh, that's not me. I would never be mad at God!" Don't be so sure. All of us get mad at God without realizing it. Think about Jonah. He has finally gotten to a place in his life where he is willing to be obedient on God's terms, but then things don't unfold according to his plan.

¹But it displeased Jonah exceedingly, and he was angry. ²And he prayed to the LORD and said, "O LORD, is not this what I said when I was yet in my country? That is why I made haste to flee to Tarshish; for I knew that you are a gracious God and merciful, slow to anger and abounding in steadfast love, and relenting from disaster. ³Therefore now, O LORD, please take my life from me, for it is better for me to die than to live." ⁴And the LORD said, "Do you do well to be angry?"

⁵Jonah went out of the city and sat to the east of the city and made a booth for himself there. He sat under it in the shade, till he should see what would become of the city.
—Jonah 4:1–5

HISTORICAL: JONAH'S ANGRY!

Sadly, Jonah's repentance after the whale incident is only temporary. When he doesn't receive the type of gratification he expects, his obedience ends.

Repentance Envy

What Jonah really wants is for God's judgment to be poured out on Nineveh. That would be awesome—for Jonah. Instead, Nineveh's miraculous, glorious, profound response frustrates the prophet. Nineveh's obedient repentance is the last thing Jonah wants. He complains, "See, Lord, I *knew* this would happen!" Jonah knows the Assyrians will hear God's message and repent, and he knows God will then spare them. In fact, he admits this is the reason he ran off to Tarshish in the first place: he knows God will end up being merciful, and he resents God for it.

Ironically, Jonah, a prophet of God, is mad at God for doing for Nineveh what God has repeatedly done for him and for Israel. Instead of being inspired by the miraculous repentance of his enemies, Jonah resents God for it. In short, he is jealous of the grace Nineveh receives. He is envious of their repentance.

Victim Hill

Jonah's hope of God wiping Nineveh out has been crushed. Now he has a new hope: that their repentance will fail (like his own has). It's a strange thing for a prophet to hope for, isn't it? Jonah finds himself a seat on what I call "Victim Hill" and is prepared to sit there for forty days so he won't miss God's judgment rolling into Nineveh.

Just think, Jonah wants Nineveh's repentance to fail so Jonah can watch God wipe out every man, woman, and child in the city. How sick is that? Of course, none of that happens. Nineveh's repentance is God-inspired and real.

Imagine being so angry and vindictive you're willing to sit on a hillside for a month in hopes that worshipers of God fail, and God judges their whole city! Jonah becomes angry with God because what Jonah wants to happen isn't part of God's plan. As Jonah camps out on Victim Hill, he forgets about his own need for grace. He has no gratitude for God's mercy in his own life.

Victim's Prayer

Pre-whale Jonah was arrogant, pathetic, passive-aggressive, selfish, and judgmental. He was mad at God. Do you remember what Jonah was praying for then? That's right, the same thing he is praying for here on Victim Hill: he wants to die.

Jonah's repentance prayer in the belly of the whale was real, and it was a beautiful prayer! But his humble, submissive, teachable moment has passed, and here on Victim Hill, he is back to pre-whale Jonah. The poor little prophet doesn't get what he wants from God, so now he doesn't even want to live anymore.

Compare Jonah's self-pitying prayer to the prayer Jesus models for us: "Your kingdom come, your will be done, on earth as it is in heaven" (Matthew 6:10). This is the last thing Jonah wants. He prefers to pray, "My will be done on earth, and I'm not worried about heaven!"

Jonah knows God won't kill him, so this is a passive-aggressive, fake, disingenuous prayer. It's victimhood, like my money-borrowing friend I mentioned earlier in the chapter declaring, "I guess I'll just starve!" Jonah can't get past what God has done, and he has no interest in serving God anymore. How did a prophet of God get here—again?

SPIRITUAL: CONFLICT WITH GOD

Jonah is now in full-on conflict with God because his desires clash with the Lord's priorities. Can you imagine what God is thinking as he watches Jonah pouting on Victim Hill, asking God to kill him?

Why Are You Angry?

If I were God, I know how I would respond to Jonah's anger and his pitiful, insincere prayer. Probably a lot like I responded to my long-lost, money-borrowing friend: "Dude, you prayed to Me from a whale, asking Me to rescue you. You promised to serve Me like a child of God should. Then I let you be the most successful preacher in human history. I used you to transform a pagan nation!

"And how do you thank Me? You squat on this ridiculous

hill, angry because I have shown them the same mercy I showed you. You are asking Me to kill you because you don't like how I do things, because I didn't wipe them out. What's wrong with you? You are a pathetic, self-absorbed, arrogant, sensitive little snowflake!" (Sorry, I got a little carried away there.)

However, God doesn't ask my advice, and He simply poses a question to Jonah, the gist of which is: "Why are you so angry? Is your anger justified?" Wow, what incredible patience God shows with these questions! They sound very much like the questions He asked Cain when Cain was angry with Him (Genesis 4:6). And God keeps being patient with Jonah afterward. His questions set up a few days of teaching moments for his prophet, which we'll explore in the next chapter.

God's Priority

> [9]*And they sang a new song, saying, "Worthy are you to take the scroll and to open its seals, for you were slain, and by your blood you ransomed people for God from every tribe and language and people and nation....*
> **—Revelation 5:9**

One of God's priorities has always been to make His kingdom the most ethnically inclusive, diverse gathering in human history. God has always intended His people to be a kingdom of priests who love and serve other people from all nations, even when they hate us. Everything else, including your most deeply held and best-intentioned earthly hopes and dreams, takes a back seat to this plan.

Jonah is mad because his priority isn't the same as God's priority. Jonah's priority is to receive mercy and grace on his terms and see Nineveh become the object of God's wrath. He wants Israel to remain the exclusive recipient of God's blessing. After all, that's why Jonah tried to run to Tarshish. He wants God's grace and mercy, but he insists God use Cash App!

Jonah is a microcosm of the whole nation of Israel at this time: a blessed nation consumed with arrogance, anger, and victimhood. Throughout the Old Testament, we see the people of Israel fulfilling their own desires, which are in direct conflict with God's priorities. They are supposed to be a blessing to all nations, but instead they have come to despise every nation apart from their own.

I believe people within the church today have this same essential conflict with God: many of our priorities don't line up with His.

PERSONAL: YOU MAD, BRO?

This chapter offers a difficult swimming lesson. The painful truth is this: it's easy to scoff at Jonah's unwillingness to embrace God's plan, but we're not so different.

Complaining or Rejoicing?

"I would never be like Jonah!" we might say. Oh, really? Often our misplaced desires and obsessions put our lives in direct conflict with God, and it's exhausting. Paul experiences this, too, as the New Testament tells us. In fact, God asks Paul a similar question to the one He asks Jonah:

> ¹⁴*And when we had all fallen to the ground, I heard a voice saying to me in the Hebrew language, "Saul, Saul, why are you persecuting me? It is hard for you to kick against the goads."*
>
> **—Acts 26:14**

Watch this. Before he meets Jesus, Paul is convinced he is zealous for God, doing righteous work, but he isn't. Even though Paul has no clue he is mad at God, the question Jesus asks him indicates his life is one giant wrestling match with God, and the early church is caught in the middle.

Later, in prison, falsely accused and facing death, with both Romans and Jews lined up against him, Paul comes to understand sincere gratitude. In fact, he writes some of the most beautiful expressions of gratitude ever. He could easily write, "Complain to the Lord always. I'll say it again: complain!" If anyone has the right to sit on Victim Hill, arms crossed, it's Paul, right? We complain about a lot less. Yet that's not what Paul says as he suffers in service to the kingdom of God. Filled with continual gratitude for God's mercy, he declares:

⁴Rejoice in the Lord always; again I will say, rejoice.
—Philippians 4:4

Which one best describes your posture toward God, complaining or rejoicing? Let's explore the possibilities.

My Victim Hill

Again, don't judge Jonah. We go to Victim Hill with God quite often without realizing it; some of us have been there for years. And I'm no exception.

At one point, I was following a story called Sermongate, about rampant plagiarism by megachurch pastors.[6] At first, I felt relieved. Thanks to all the work I put into my sermons each week, I didn't have to feel guilty about such a scandal. But then I grew frustrated, even angry. How could all these lazy, plagiarizing pastors have such big churches? Why didn't they get what they deserved? Why didn't people appreciate (my) arduous work in writing sermons?

I will be the first to admit that way of thinking is twisted. What's more, though it seemed like my frustration was with other pastors or with church people, I later realized my real frustration was with God. *"Why, God, are You using undeserving pastors and churches?"* I wondered in my heart. *"My church deserves better. We've earned it!"* Do you see how easy it is to fall into this trap of being mad at God? I'd say I was even worse than Jonah, mired in my jealousy of other pastors.

After a few days, I heard God asking me a question: "Joe, why are you angry? Is it justified? I have given you the incredible privilege of preaching to a precious group of My children every Sunday!" I had lapsed into ingratitude for the undeserved privilege and blessing of preaching for my church family each week.

> ²⁴*Then Jesus told his disciples, "If anyone would come after me, let him deny himself and take up his cross and follow me. ²⁵For whoever would save his life will lose it, but whoever loses his life for my sake will find it."*
> **—Matthew 16:24–25**

We all, like Jonah, have these "crosses" Jesus speaks of. We all have those dark places where we love some things more than we love our Savior and His kingdom. Sometimes they are hard to spot because, on the surface, they can seem like righteous places! These obsessions corrupt our priorities, pulling them out of line with God's priorities. These are the things we feel so entitled to we lose our sense of gratitude for the mercy and grace God has given us.

Maybe for you, it's a passionate feeling or belief about what God should be doing in your life, your community, or your country. Maybe it's about personal financial success, or perhaps you believe you deserve a better spouse or kids. It could be obvious or very subtle. It could seem like righteous anger, like mine did. These are rough seas of disobedience to swim in.

23Search me, O God, and know my heart! Try me and know my thoughts! 24And see if there be any grievous way in me, and lead me in the way everlasting!

—Psalm 139:23–24

Have no doubt: all of us struggle with being mad at God at some point in life, and we usually don't even realize it. It takes some deep introspection to recognize when anger with God creeps into your heart. So, how can you know if you're angry at God?

If you are willing to swim into these waters with me, let's look at the following checklist for signs you're mad at God. It always starts with a feeling of entitled discontent, like God owes you more. Ask yourself:

- Am I so disappointed I have lost the desire to be actively involved in advancing God's kingdom?

- Am I so frustrated I have pulled back from my relationship with God and His church?

- Am I so mad I can go months without serving others or being with God's people?

- Am I so upset I have abandoned full repentance somewhere along the way?

- Am I so discontented I cannot remember the last time I read the Bible or prayed for someone else?

Be honest: are you sitting on Victim Hill, with your arms crossed, upset because God isn't giving you what you want? Perhaps God is asking you today, "Why are you so angry with Me?" Let's take His question seriously.

Chapter Six Questions

Question: Have you ever been angry at God or frustrated with how He does things? What was the result, and what did you learn? Is there still more you can learn from that situation?

_____

_____

_____

_____

_____

_____

_____

_____

_____

_____

_____

_____

Question: Are there any misplaced desires and obsessions in your life that put you in conflict with God? What are these things? Why do you hang on to them? What adjustments can you make to start bringing your life into alignment with God's priorities?

_____

_____

_____

_____

_____

_____

_____

_____

_____

_____

Question: What best describes your posture toward God, complaining or rejoicing? Why? What examples from your life capture this reality? If your life is more characterized by complaining, what steps can you take to pursue a life of rejoicing?

_____

_____

_____

_____

_____

_____

_____

_____

_____

_____

_____

Action: Review the assessment in this chapter to evaluate if you're angry at God. In a notebook, a journal, or on a piece of paper, answer the questions asked in the assessment. Ask God to help you be humble and honest in your responses, and allow Him to show you any hidden areas of anger or victimhood. Then plead with Him to change your heart.

Chapter Six Notes

_____

_____

_____

_____

_____

_____

_____

_____

_____

_____

_____

_____

_____

_____

_____

_____

Listening to God

Have you ever asked someone a question and, even though you know the person heard you, he or she didn't answer? How did you feel? Did it seem like the person was choosing not to listen, intentionally ignoring you? Did you feel disrespected? How did you respond?

For my part, I want to assure you I am infinitely patient. Such is my overflowing compassion that my first inclination is to caress the other person's suffering brow and ask, "What's wrong? How can I help?"

Of course, I am quite the opposite, as most of us are. We are more likely to become impatient with the other person, repeat ourselves, increase our volume, and possibly add some "linguistic flavor" to our phrasing.

Imagine if, when we ignore God's word, He were to treat us the same way we treat people who ignore us. How often do you hear truth from a sermon or from reading Scripture and ignore it, rationalizing away its relevance? Maybe you consistently ignore biblical truth about money, the kingdom of heaven, loving one another, immoral behavior, or unhealthy relationships. This is Jonah's problem as well: from the beginning, he refuses to listen, ignoring the Lord's instruction.

Do you believe you're good at listening to God, knowing when He is speaking and what He is saying? Learning how to listen to God is one of the most difficult swimming lessons any Christian can learn. Do we *really* want to hear God's words, even if we find them inconvenient, costly, or unpleasant? It seems like Jonah doesn't.

> ⁶Now the LORD God appointed a plant and made it come up over Jonah, that it might be a shade over his head, to save him from his discomfort. So Jonah was exceedingly glad because of the plant. ⁷But when dawn came up the next day, God appointed a worm that attacked the plant, so that it withered. ⁸When the sun rose, God appointed a scorching east wind, and the sun beat down on the head of Jonah so that he was faint. And he asked that he might die and said, "It is better for me to die than to live." ⁹But God said to Jonah, "Do you do well to be angry for the plant?" And he said, "Yes, I do well to be angry, angry enough to die." ¹⁰And the LORD said, "You pity the plant, for which you did not labor, nor did you make it grow, which came into being in a night and perished in a night. ¹¹And should not I pity Nineveh, that great city, in which there are more than 120,000 persons who do not know their right hand from their left, and also much cattle?"
>
> **—Jonah 4:6–11**

HISTORICAL: JONAH IGNORES GOD

My favorite feature of many text-messaging platforms is the notice you receive if someone has read your message. If the person reads it but doesn't respond, I start wondering, "Are they too busy to reply? Are they angry at me? Am I not important enough to them?" Usually, I follow up with an entirely godly, humble, compassionate row of fifteen question marks. If I get the notification that the person has read this message as well, but he or she still doesn't say anything, I become filled with "righteous anger."

In this last part of the story, the prophet doesn't do much, except ignore a clear question from God. God has already asked Jonah why he is upset about Nineveh receiving God's mercy: "Do you do well to be angry?" (Jonah 4:4).

Jonah hears God's question, and God knows Jonah hears Him, but Jonah chooses not to answer. What gall, to deliberately ignore the Lord! This might be a worse offense than refusing to go to Nineveh in the first place. God's response to Jonah's non-answer becomes the focus of the rest of the chapter.

SPIRITUAL: PATIENT CONVERSATION

We've seen God's persistent mercy and patience with Jonah. God goes to great lengths to bring Jonah to a place where he will finally be willing to listen. Now, over the next forty-eight hours, God displays even more grace to Jonah by speaking to him again, this time in four compassionate ways.

Comforting Gourd

Overnight, God grows a plant large enough to shade Jonah from the hot Assyrian sun. The King James Bible translates the word *plant* as "gourd" (Jonah 4:6 KJV). Since a gourd can take almost six months to grow to maturity, [7] Jonah has to know this rapid-growing gourd is God's work. Once God comforts Jonah with the shade, Jonah instantly stops praying God will kill him.

Jonah is obviously glad for the shade, but unfortunately his appreciation stops there. Without any expression of gratitude or humility, Jonah simply consumes the blessing. You would think a comforting, miraculous blessing such as this would get Jonah's attention: *"Wow, God is so gracious to me!"* But no, Jonah enjoys his newfound, unearned comfort from God with no concern for the fact that he doesn't really deserve it.

Hungry Worm

Then, after one day of shade, God sends an incredibly hungry worm, which kills the gourd overnight—botanical miracle number two! Surely, the sudden death of this super-plant, which is large enough to shade Jonah from the oppressive heat, will grab his attention: *"Hmm, God is trying to tell me something here. I should probably listen."* Yet Jonah wakes up and says nothing.

Scorching Wind

With Jonah's shade come and gone and the prophet still refusing to respond, God brings on a heat wave. Jonah, by his own choice, now sits on top of Victim Hill, baking in the brutally hot sun. The rational action would be to come down from Victim Hill when it becomes so unbearable. Instead, Jonah returns to his self-pitying victim prayer: "God, just kill me." *Really Jonah?* After everything Jonah has been through, all the grace and mercy God has shown him, Jonah ends up right back where he was on the ship.

This is the third time Jonah has prayed this prayer. If I were God, I would be quite annoyed by Jonah's whole deal. Jonah's repeated request that God kill him reveals an odd cycle of dysfunction in Jonah's relationship with the Lord. (Can you relate?) Once again, Jonah is sulking in circumstances of his own making and blaming God for them.

To me, the most remarkable part of this story is how God doesn't answer Jonah's frequent request and kill this chronically disobedient prophet! God never plans to judge Jonah the way Jonah deserves to be judged. Instead, God remains in relentless pursuit of Jonah. God is determined to teach, shepherd, and transform Jonah into who God wants him to be.

God Gets the Last Word

This seems like a lot of hassle for God, going through all this trouble to redeem an ingrate like Jonah. Why does God even bother? In a word, *grace*. After enduring all of Jonah's bitterness and sporadic obedience, after providing an ungrateful Jonah with comfort, after sustaining him during his suffering pity party, God has now cornered Jonah with grace, and he has no way to escape it. God has patiently shepherded Jonah circumstantially, physically, emotionally, and intellectually into a beautiful mercy trap, with no way out!

All the episodes in Jonah's story—the boat, the storm, the whale, a repentant Nineveh, the shade plant, the ravenous worm, and the heat—are manifestations of God's patience and grace toward Jonah. The Lord uses all of it to show Jonah the foolish, irrational, and ridiculous nature of his anger and selective moral outrage. All of this culminates in God's final question to Jonah, which underscores, once again, God's patience and mercy.

"Jonah, you're upset about a plant you had nothing to do with, but you don't care about the 120,000 children in Nineveh? You're more upset about a gourd than thousands of cattle, which actually feel pain? Do you see how irrational this is?"

This is the climax of the story, yet nothing more is written. That's where the book of Jonah ends. It's a "drop the mic" moment for God, and there is nothing left for Jonah to say. The prophet is so stunned by God's question that when he later records the story in this book for others to read for thousands of years, Jonah lets the Lord have the final word. God's mercy brings him to a beautiful moment in which he has no choice but to zip his lips and listen. The book of Job ends the same way. When God speaks, there is never anything else to be said.

PERSONAL: TIME TO LISTEN

Our patient, loving Father knows we can be hard of hearing and short of memory, often needing Him to repeat things. Most of the time, we're either unable or unwilling to hear what God is saying to us. It becomes a constant struggle. We know what God's word says about what obedience looks like in the different areas of life, but we choose to ignore His loving warnings. Why is God so patient with people who regularly ignore His word? Why go to all the trouble?

> *⁶And I am sure of this, that he who began a good work in you will bring it to completion at the day of Jesus Christ.*
> *—Philippians 1:6*

This passage explains why God goes through all the hassle with Jonah and with us. Even if you spend most of your time ignoring what you know is right, God relentlessly pursues you. He has an insatiable desire to corner us with mercy and grace, giving us no alternative but to turn to Him. God will not let anything hinder the transformation of His beloved, chosen children, not even our own stubborn, irrational, arrogant disobedience! Knowing this is God's intention for you, are you prepared to learn how to listen?

Blessing and Suffering

We often misinterpret things God does as a response to what *we* have done or are not doing. Do we think Jonah deserves the blessing of the miracle gourd's shade? Of course, he doesn't; he is being disobedient. But Jonah deserves the scorching heat, right? Wrong—he deserves much worse! None of Jonah's story, from the storm and the whale to the worm and the heat, is about what he deserves.

How often do we misinterpret what we experience as something we deserve, as blessings or punishment? It requires a great deal of human arrogance for any of us to believe we deserve the comfort of a shady gourd or whatever our equivalent blessing may be. Usually when we receive blessings from God, we conveniently forget to ask what God is actually doing. Instead, we simply thank Him and enjoy consuming what we have received. We assume the reason we are being blessed is that, somewhere along the line, we listened to God and obeyed Him so well we've obliged Him to show us favor.

Suffering, however, is a whole different ball game. "What have I done to deserve this?" we complain. "Why is God letting this happen?" Again, consider the human arrogance required to assume someone who is suffering is being punished by God. If we don't think we need as much grace as Jonah or Nineveh, if not more, then we haven't been listening to God very well. Do we mean to say we don't deserve hardship, but others in this world do?

Personally, I think it seems silly to believe God spends His time playing whack-a-mole or Santa Claus with His children. Doesn't it make more sense to take God at His word and believe He is actually focused on making sure His good work is completed in us? God isn't punishing you or rewarding you. He is talking to you, coaxing your rebellious heart into a mercy and grace trap!

Chapter Seven Questions

Question: How often do you hear truth in a sermon or from Scripture and end up ignoring it or rationalizing away its relevance? Is there a truth in God's word you are aware of that you're currently refusing to apply to your life? Why are you choosing to ignore it? What do you think will be the outcome of ignoring it?

_____

_____

_____

_____

_____

_____

_____

_____

_____

_____

_____

Question: Do you believe you're good at listening to God, knowing when He is speaking and what He is saying? Why or why not? Do you genuinely desire to hear God and obey Him? How can you develop this skill?

_____

_____

_____

_____

_____

_____

_____

_____

_____

_____

Question: Are there lessons from God in your life that have needed continual repetition for you to understand and implement them in a lasting way? What can you learn about God and His love for you through the patience He shows you? Why do you think God goes through the trouble of trying to teach you? How will this perspective impact how you respond to God's future attempts to teach you?

_____

_____

_____

_____

_____

_____

_____

_____

_____

_____

_____

Action: On a piece of paper, draw two columns. Title one column, "Reward," and the other column, "Punishment." In each column, list different circumstances or events in your life you would label either rewards or punishments. Then evaluate those events from the perspective that God is using all things to complete His work in you. How does this change your perspective on the experiences you placed in each column? How will it impact your view of your life circumstances moving forward?

Chapter Seven Notes

_____

_____

_____

_____

_____

_____

_____

_____

_____

_____

_____

_____

_____

_____

Break the Cycle

> Sometimes, God puts us through unusual experiences in order that we may the better understand him; and sometimes that we may the better know ourselves. Men who are of a hard nature must have hard usage, diamond must cut diamond, that at last the purpose of the great Owner of the jewels may be accomplished. [8]
>
> **—Charles Spurgeon**

If we're sincere, we will admit we are a lot like Jonah. Willful disobedience to God causes our lives to become a constant, self-destructive cycle of dysfunction. God is speaking to you today, like He was speaking to Jonah. In fact, it is possible God has been patiently trying to get your attention for a while now. Perhaps, like Jonah, you have had moments of temporary spiritual lucidity, but you still haven't learned to be quiet and listen to God. We can spend years praying misguided prayers, wishing God would do something we want. There seems to be no answer, but the real problem isn't that God doesn't hear us; it's that our listening skills aren't what they should be.

What are some areas of your life where you have been refusing to listen to God? Money? Personal purity? Ministry or service? In one way or another, He is likely asking you to let go of something you're reluctant to surrender. I hope studying the story of Jonah in this book has given you a mirror to help you see your spiritual dysfunction, along with instructions for breaking the cycle of dysfunction between you and God.

The key now is not to procrastinate. Begin today to break your cycle of dysfunction by learning to swim in obedience to God, by His grace. Our study of Jonah has provided several important swimming lessons to help us do this:

- We learned how we often tend to hoard the grace God has given us, becoming obsessed with our own little world as we run from obedience.

- We learned we cannot hide from God, no matter how hard we try, because His love and sovereign grace will keep coming for us.

- We learned grace is designed for people just like us, people who think we know best even though we do not.

- We learned what real confession and true repentance look like.

- We learned how understanding and fearing God's judgment are crucial to repentance.

- We learned how to know when we are mad at God and about all the dangerous consequences that come with this heart posture toward the Lord.

- We learned how God will constantly use circumstances, both good and bad, to speak to us—and to corner us in a mercy trap!

Through each of these lessons, we discovered how easily we can become like Jonah, maybe without even realizing it. Above all, we learned the story of Jonah isn't about a whale, but about God's relentless love for His chosen people.

As we apply these swimming lessons, we will learn how to experience God's love in ways we never knew possible, and we will come to see obedience to God as a privilege. Obedience is a blessing, not a burden!

Perhaps today, God is having a "mic drop" moment with you, leaving you with nothing to say but *"Wow!"* Do you know what that is? Like Jonah's account, it's a story of grace, mercy, redemption, and forgiveness. It's the gospel taking hold in your heart!

God is speaking to us today, which means it's time for us to shut up and listen. It's time we let Him have the last word.

About the Author

Joe is the founding pastor of GraceLife Church (www.gracelifesrq.com) in Sarasota, Florida. He holds a Doctor of Divinity, a master's degree in theology, a bachelor's degree in biblical studies, and another in pastoral studies.

After beginning vocational ministry at age 18, Joe spent his first twenty-two years of ministry as a youth pastor and an outreach pastor in three different churches. He coached high school football and basketball for nearly twenty years.

In 2008, Joe founded Mobilepreacher.org (www.mobilepreacher.org), an organization designed to help seasoned ministers create ministries that might not fit inside traditional church walls. He is also the founder and executive director of the Nightlife Center in Sarasota (www.nightlifecenter.org) and the author of *The GraceLife: What Philippians Teaches Us About Loving One Another*

Relentlessly and *Surviving in Egypt: The Life of Joseph*.

Joe is husband to Laura and father to Ben. You can find him on Twitter (@mobilepreacher), Instagram (Mobilepreacher), and Facebook (facebook.com/Mobilepreacher).

About Renown Publishing

Renown Publishing was founded with one mission in mind: to make your great idea famous.

At Renown Publishing, we don't just publish. We work hard to pair strategy with innovative marketing techniques so that your book launch is the start of something bigger.

Learn more at RenownPublishing.com.

Notes

1. "Introduction to Jonah." ESV.org. https://www.esv.org/resources/esv-global-study-bible/introduction-to-jonah/.

2. "Introduction to Jonah," ESV.org.

3. "Introduction to Jonah," ESV.org.

4. "Afflictions of Assyria Against Israel." ESV.org. https://www.esv.org/resources/esv-global-study-bible/chart-34-01/.

5. Hobson, Tom. "Jonah and the Eclipse in Ancient Nineveh." Patheos. August 7, 2017. https://www.patheos.com/blogs/tomhobson/2017/08/jonah-eclipse-ancient-nineveh/.

6. Mayer, Emma. "Pastor Ed Litton Compared to Nixon as Plagiarism Battle Rages in Southern Baptist Convention." *Newsweek.* July 3, 2021. https://www.newsweek.com/pastor-ed-litton-compared-nixon-plagiarism-battle-rages-southern-baptist-convention-1606688.

7. Palm Healing Lite. "How Long Does It Take for a Gourd to Grow?" 2022. https://gumbokrewe.com/how-long-does-it-take-for-a-gourd-to-grow/#:~:text=Gourds%20are%20planted%20in%20spring%2C%20as%20soon%20as,up%20to%20180%20days%20after%20planting.Sep%208%2C%202021.

8. Spurgeon, Charles Haddon. "Jonah's Object-Lessons." The Spurgeon Center. June 11, 1885. https://www.spurgeon.org/resource-library/sermons/jonahs-object-lessons/#flipbook/.